PONYCRAFT

The Byerly Turk

*No hour of life is lost
that is spent in the saddle*

PONYCRAFT

written and illustrated by
ANNE BULLEN

LONDON
BLANDFORD PRESS

First published 1956
Second impression 1959
Revised edition 1963
Reprinted 1965
Revised edition 1969
Reprinted 1972

© 1963 Blandford Press Ltd,
167 High Holborn, London WC1V 6PH

ISBN 0 7137 0162 5

DEDICATION

To the good companions
Anthony, Michael, Charlie,
Jenny, Jane and Sarah

Printed in Great Britain by
Jarrold and Sons Ltd, Norwich

CONTENTS

★

The Arab Legend (see page 8)

The Eohippus

CHAPTER ONE

The History of Our Horses

I OFTEN wonder how many people pause to think of the wonder and romance of the past history of our horses.

"In the beginning God created the heavens and the earth," and millions of years ago in the Eocene Age emerged the five-toed mammal which is the ancestor of our horse.

Only about the size of a fox, it is called by scientists the "Eohippus"; it had five toes, like the fingers and thumb on a man's hand, and it ran on four of them.

After ten million years the horse, now the size of a sheep, ran on three toes. It is called the "Mesohippus". This not-so-hand-some ancestor was followed in about another ten million years by the "Merychippus", an animal the size of an ass, possessing the three toes, but running only on one of them.

At the end of the Pleistocene Age, which ended twenty-five million years ago, we have the hoofed pony covered with hair, looking rather like the ponies found in Siberia today. The toes had at last become hoofs, and the second and fourth toes had become the splint bones, thus following nature's law that what is not used is taken away.

The Eohippus

The origins of many of the different breeds of horses are still wrapped in obscurity; but it must be from these tough little ponies of Asia that the small wiry horse of Atilla and the Norsemen came.

The Arab has a lovely legend about its origin. "When Allah willed to create the horse, he said to the south wind, 'Condense thyself; I will that a creature should proceed from thee!' Then came the angel Gabriel who took a handful of this matter and presented it to Allah, who formed of it a dark bay and a dark chestnut horse."

We know that Arab horses existed thousands of years before Christ. There are drawings of them in ancient Egypt and in China years before the great flood. The record of their service to man is almost as old as history.

Hagar's son, Ishmael, raised a famous stud of Arab horses, much prized in later years by Solomon who, we are told, kept forty thousand stalls for his chariot horses.

Can we picture this number of horses today? It almost takes our breath away to think of them. All down the ages horses have followed man's history, and

The Mesohippus

8

for well over two thousand years B.C., we can trace them through China, Assyria and Egypt to Greece and Rome. In Greece in 680 B.C. at the twenty-third Olympiad, the horse made his first appearance at the games; a few years later he was driven in the famous chariot races. In Rome the races took place in the circus, a large round arena. Horse-racing was run on much the same lines as our races today. But though the corruption would have given our jockey club many a headache, the racing encouraged the breeding and importing of swift and lovely horses.

By then the Moors from Africa were masters of Spain; they were keen breeders, having imported Barb and Arab horses into the country. Many of these lovely horses came to gallop in the circus at Rome.

The Merychippus

When the barbarians invaded Rome, Alaric the Visegot and Attila the Hun left behind many of their sturdy, hardy ponies; these were bred to the Roman horses and were the forerunners of the war horse of the middle ages.

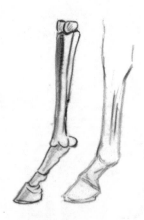

The Merychippus   The Modern Horse

9

In Britain, generations of Norsemen had left behind their tough little ponies, which rather resembled the Exmoor ponies of today. It was these ponies, pulling warriors in wicker chariots, that confronted Caesar when he landed in Britain in A.D. 54.

We learn from our history books that Alfred the Great burnt the cakes and founded the British Navy; but we do not learn about his keenness for horse breeding, and how he created the post of Horse Thane, whose duties were to manage his horses and carry out his mandates on breeding and stable management.

Following this came Athelstone in A.D. 925, in whose reign

The Norseman

The Chariot Race

horse dealing became a vast commercial project. Laws were made to protect people from fraud in horse dealing, and to punish the miscreants.

We may forget some of the dull things about William the Conqueror in 1066, but surely we must remember that he brought with him a magnificent black Spanish stallion, which he rode throughout his victorious progress.

As hunting was the great sport of the Normans, many fine horses were imported, and breeding was much encouraged.

During the reign of Henry II, a weekly sale was held at Smithfield and this was a great sight, according to the historian. Jousts and competitions took place, horses were bought and sold. In fact, the occasion was a mixture of a horse show and the old weekly Tattersalls!

Then followed the era of the "great horse". Many horses were imported from Flanders, while the Crusaders brought back others from the East. All our kings encouraged horse breeding, for horses meant wealth, until finally, in the reign of the Tudors, laws were made restricting size and breeding. One law that was enforced was that all entire horses were to be stabled or "stalled", hence the term "stallion" or stalled one.

Henry VIII ordered all stallions under 13 h.h. to be destroyed, also youngsters or, as he called them, "unlikely tits", who at two years old were not over 11.2 h.h. This order cleared the moors and hills of many ponies.

James I, with his gunpowder and firearms, found no use for heavy horses, so they were bred lighter and faster by introducing Eastern blood again. Horse racing now became popular. Van Dyke's lovely pictures of Charles I show the beautiful type of horse the kings rode.

In George I's reign, and in Georgian times, riding schools became the vogue; possibly it was the turn for the dressage enthusiasts. Arab and Barb blood was introduced; the Byerley Turk came in 1687, the famous Darley Arabian was brought from Allepo in 1720, followed by the Godolphin Arabian in 1787. These famous horses are the ancestors of our modern thoroughbred, which is now world-famous.

Assyrian Horses

The Great Horse

Then what about our ponies? Much nonsense is talked about our *pure* native breeds when, as we know, to produce a set breed and to improve these ponies, people have crossed other blood into them for hundreds of years. For instance, in the reign of Henry I, Roger de Belesne, Earl of Shrewsbury, introduced a Spanish stallion on to his estate at Powisland to "improve" the Welsh ponies.

Poor keep and hard conditions have kept these animals small, and selection and judicious out crossing from time to time have preserved for us the heritage of our nine native breeds of ponies. It is from these that we now breed our lovely show ponies, crossing them with Arab and thoroughbred.

The result is often a perfect miniature of a large horse, some resembling thoroughbred, some Arab, and those with more substance miniature hunters.

But whenever we look back into the past, we see horses and ponies the friends and servants of man. Sometimes over-burdened, killed in battle, or worn out in the shafts, they are still, as they have always been, man's faithful companions.

Shall we travel on into the next life without meeting them on the journey? Personally I do not think so. Did not God Himself honour the stable on that first Christmas night?

The Darley Arabian

13

CHAPTER TWO

Buying a Pony

THIS is a most exciting moment—having a pony of your own. Try to know first exactly what you want, and then go to someone who has a good name in the dealing world and ask for help to find it. If you like, before going to your dealer friend, make local inquiries about something suitable. You may be lucky and able to acquire something that you know to be a good pony and that the owner has outgrown. If that is the case, go over and try the pony and, if you like it, ask to have it vetted before buying it—and may you have all the fun and good luck with it.

If you fail to find something locally, go to a dealer you know has a good reputation. Tell him what you want and ask him how much you should have to pay for it—then wait for him to find the right pony for you. When he finds one, try the pony well and, if you decide you like it, have it vetted and pay for it when you go and fetch it. Don't do as many people do—ask a dealer to get you a pony and say you will leave it to him, and then go off and get fixed up through a friend elsewhere. This naturally makes the dealer fed up with you, and if you are unfortunate and find you are stuck with a bad one through a friend's ignorant recommendation, you cannot then return to the dealer and expect him to take any interest. If you play straight with a reputable dealer he will

Why *is it being sold?*

be straight with you; but don't treat him as if he were a possible
rogue and you the local smart guy!

Unfortunately there are many rogues in the horse trade, as in
many other trades, and women are often more unscrupulous
than men. Some appear to have no conscience and will sell
dangerous animals as reliable ponies for children. Such practices
are unforgiveable and I cannot think that it can really be worth
while as they must lose many good customers.

Many strange things happen in horse dealing, and the cheap
pony cleverly picked up at a sale may not be cheap in the long
run. It is possible to drug a pony to make it quiet for twenty-
four hours, to cocain a lame leg so that, when you come to try

A pony of your own

it, it is sound; to doctor his wind so that, temporarily, it doesn't make a noise—and very many other things too numerous to mention. One of the foremost is dyeing. The dye soon wears off and you probably see a hideous white blaze emerging! We once bought a horse from a rogue and, though dead quiet with traffic when we tried him, he proved in reality to be really dangerous when the drug had worn off. It was our own fault for going to a man with a doubtful reputation. Still, a lesson or two is good for one and teaches one to be more careful in future.

The sort of questions to ask when you go to look at a pony are: Its age, and breeding. Why is it being sold? (You may of course *not* get the true reason!) Is it quiet in the stable and with traffic? Is it easy to catch in the field? Has it been hunted by a child? If so, when and where?

See it measured if possible, especially if you want it for showing classes—or tell your vet to be very exact in his measurement when he vets it for you. For showing, $\frac{1}{2}$ in. can make a difference of hundreds of pounds in its value. Hence all the villainy practised over measuring horses. On the other hand, if you are not buying a pony for showing, $\frac{1}{2}$ in. over the showing class heights is of no importance, and an animal of 14.3 h.h. is often far cheaper than a 14.2$\frac{1}{2}$ h.h. pony which can be shown in the 14.2$\frac{1}{2}$ h.h. classes. The usual show classes are divided into 12.2 h.h. and under, 13.2 h.h. and under, and 14.2 h.h. and under. Half an inch is always allowed for shoes so that they may become $\frac{1}{2}$ in. over these heights when shod—but *no* more!

Some people are hopeless

CHAPTER THREE

You and Your Young Pony

ANIMALS know the people who love and understand them, just as children do; and as one person can control a class of children without difficulty, while with another the class is pandemonium, so it is with the control of animals.

Remember, quietness, firmness and gentleness are essential in handling young animals. Like children they must first be taught obedience. To be led, to be tied up, and to do what they are told quietly and without fuss, are the first lessons.

But before trying to teach your pony, you yourself must learn all you can, otherwise you *and your young pony* will be very much at sea. There is an art even in catching a pony. Some people are hopeless and the most friendly pony won't let them catch him.

The first rule is never to approach the horse from the front. Go up to his near side shoulder and stand with your back to his tail. Feed him with your left hand and, talking to him all the time, put your right arm round his neck, take the rope end from your left hand and hold it round his neck. Then slip the noose over his nose and up over his ears. You can then release your neck rope and lead him away. Never forget your tit-bits when catching a horse and you will seldom have any trouble.

If you buy a pony that is difficult to catch, leave the head collar on him and tie a short piece of rope to dangle under his jaw. This you can quietly get hold of when he is sniffing at your other hand. If the pony is really bad to catch you will have to put a long trailing rope on him and start by turning him out in a bare yard, where he will become very bored with little to eat; then if you have a nice tit-bit or small feed for him whenever you come near him, he will soon be delighted to see you. Always leave him wanting more, and to start with just feed him and pat him and leave him. After a week in such a boring situation, try him in a larger area, still with the trailing rope; and when he always welcomes you, then turn him out in your larger field. When leading your youngster, do be careful *never* to wrap the rope round your hand. Loop your long rein from the knot towards the horse. Two people may be necessary if a youngster has not been led before, to drive him on or help to restrain him.

19

Hold it round his neck

Make him obey your orders, to whoa, walk, trot, and canter. Teach him to stand correctly in a balanced manner, and then this habit of standing properly will be formed for life. It is a dreadful job teaching a pony to stand and make the best of himself, when he has never learned to do so in his youth.

To tie up is perhaps the first lesson in real discipline. But never tie up a youngster and go off and leave him "to get on with it", as I have heard some people do.

The first lesson in real discipline

To tie your young pony up use a halter, a good strong halter, not your best head collar which he may break. Tie a string on to your halter and tie the pony up to a strong rail with a safety bow, i.e. a form of knot that can be pulled undone. While he is tied up keep an eye on him. Don't worry if he fidgets or stands on his hind legs, after a week he will learn to stand quietly and he has then learnt lesson one.

I personally have all my ponies tied up for "stables", and have proved that it is better for them and for the pupils who are learning to look after them.

Teach your pony to pick his feet up when you tap his leg and speak to him, to "come over" in the stable when you ask him and in general to be a charming mannerly companion.

Brush over your youngster every day, as it helps to handle him; if he is nervous and you start gently and quietly he will soon get used to being handled.

Punishment is a difficult subject for the inexperienced. Personally I always correct a horse if he kicks or bites, and I speak sharply to him as well. Very soon I find he learns that, whatever he has done with his previous owner, he may not kick or bite with me. But first you must understand that kicking is a natural reaction from fear, and if you get kicked by a nervous youngster the correct treatment is not to hit him as you would an older pony.

If you are looking after your own pony, work out a routine for yourself and stick to it. Don't feed him when you feel like it, or worse still forget to feed him more often than not.

There are some golden rules about feeding and there are many technical books about stable management. But the basic principles are:

Water before you feed.

Feed little and often, if possible.

THE CHIEF FEEDING STUFFS ARE:

Oats, best fed crushed or rolled as they are easier to digest.

Bran, good broad bran is best, containing plenty of flour; damp slightly to feed, or give as

Bran mash, useful to help digestion for a tired horse, acts as a laxative; boiled linseed and 1 tablespoonful Epsom Salts may be added and given once a week.

Horse nuts are an excellent balanced ration for horses and are not so heating as oats, but they are very expensive.

Chaff, chopped hay added to feeds makes bulk.

Feeding Table for pony of 14.2 h.h., ridden by child of thirteen, approx. per day:

oats	*bran*	*chaff*
5 lb.	5 lb.	Double handful per feed.

YOUR GROOM KIT SHOULD CONSIST OF:

1 Dandy brush for brushing off the mud and sweat.

1 Body brush for grooming your pony and cleaning his coat.

1 Curry comb for cleaning the body brush.

1 Wisp of hay or straw for massaging the pony.

1 Water brush for damping the mane or tail.

1 Stable rubber.

1 Hoof pick.

1 Sponge.

1 Mane comb.

A word of warning about tails

A word of warning about tails: do not dandy brush them out or comb them. A body brush is the right brush for cleaning the tail, and the wrong treatment will result in there being no long hair left, which is very ugly. Wash your pony's mane and tail regularly and rinse them well, using a good shampoo.

Never use detergents, whatever your friends may say. They are all excellent things for their own purpose, but they can cause trouble and irritation of the skin and give you a lot of bother.

Never wet the tail bandage; it may shrink when on the pony and get too tight.

Be careful to take your tail bandage off at night; if it is tight enough to stay on all night it is bad for the tail, and if not it will come off and be soiled or lost in the bedding.

If your pony lives out, as most ponies do these days, see that he has adequate protection from the sun and flies in summer and a good water supply, and in winter shelter of some kind, even if only a thick hedge.

Give hay when the grass has all gone, from the end of December especially. If you are hunting him he will need corn too.

I know people who will hunt cheerfully all day on their grass-fed pony, staying out till hounds go home, and will then turn the pony out with no feed into a bare paddock and rush indoors and eat an enormous tea themselves.

Such behaviour is neither humane nor is it good horse management. Well fed and with good shelter your pony can, however, live out in all weathers.

Your clipped and stabled pony is far more difficult, and after hunting will need care to prevent him getting chilled and to make him comfortable. After the worst mud has been brushed off or rubbed off with straw, he needs flannel bandages on his legs to keep him warm and to dry off his legs if they are wet. His ears

Rigged up for the night

and chest must be dried, and if he is wet from rain or sweat put straw or hay under his rug to allow the passage of air. Usually a chilled drink and a bran mash are given, and another feed later on when the pony is dry and the rest of the mud has been brushed off, and he is rigged up for the night. The morning after hunting, lead your pony out to unstiffen him and see if he is sound.

★   ★   ★

Your "tack", as your saddle and bridle is called, will be an important item and possibly an expensive one.

Try first to go to some sales and pick up some saddlery bargains. But check over the leather carefully, for it is useless and dangerous to buy rotten leather. Your saddle, to fit properly, must clear the withers in front and the spine behind. The bridle must fit your pony comfortably, and the diagram will show you the points to look for.

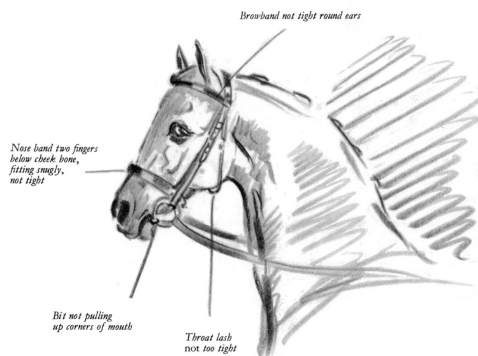

Browband not tight round ears

Nose band two fingers below cheek bone, fitting snugly, not tight

Bit not pulling up corners of mouth

Throat lash not too tight

It is correct to have bits stitched on to bridles, also the reins; buckles are incorrect, billeted bridles are neat and may be used.

| Eggbut Snaffle | Half Moon Pelham | Bridoon Bit | Weymouth Bit used with bridoon for double bridle |

Let your pony wear the bit that suits him. A jointed snaffle is the most usual bit, but some ponies need more leverage, and a pelham or double bridle are necessary.

The pressure of the bit should act on the bars of the mouth as with a curb bit; the jointed snaffle has nutcracker action and also acts on the corners of the mouth. Some horses have a larger, thicker tongue which is not comfortable with a straight bit lying across it; a port on the bit allows more room and may be more comfortable. There are many other variations of the snaffle and curb bits; as a basic principle, aim at using the least severe bit possible for control, and the thicker the mouthpiece of the bit the more comfortable it is for the pony. Use a martingale with a young, green pony in a snaffle, either a standing or running martingale. If you use the latter, be sure to use stops on your reins. A martingale gives you more control and though the pony which is really well schooled should not need one, it is a great help to the less well schooled, and the neck straps can be invaluable for the rider!

Remember that you can get a very ordinary-looking pony to do great things if you are prepared to work and take a lot of trouble.

If you wish to show, the class is for the most beautiful, and you must not feel disgruntled if a more beautiful pony beats yours! The pony must also be going perfectly on that day. A show pony is always judged on the day's form, or should be.

Everyone, however, can have an equal chance of success in the Pony Club events. Looks and height are immaterial, and there are jumping competitions, hunter trials, riding tests and even the coveted Pony Club inter-branch team event to work for. For all these things your pony must be able to jump *well* and freely and to enjoy it. As I have written a chapter on jumping, I will say no more about this here.

He must also learn to move well, with a correct carriage and rhythm, and to obey the aids correctly. When he understands all this he may learn to do turns on the forehand and haunches, changes of leg, and movements on two tracks.

There is no end to the interesting and fascinating things you can learn and do, if you are lucky enough to own a pony, but you must possess keenness, and enthusiasm, and not mind hard work.

With a correct carriage

CHAPTER FOUR

The Health of your Pony

I THINK a word here would not be out of place on condition and stable care.

Most horses, as well as dogs, suffer from parasites or
"worms", which live in the stomach and intestines. These
parasites live on the host's nourishment and therefore prevent the
animal making full use of its food and so getting into condition.

To be sure that you start right, always give your pony a
three-week course of "worm powders" in spring and autumn,
and when you buy a new pony, do this before anything else.
Consult your vet, or buy a good powder from a veterinary
chemist. Mix the powder into a small, tasty feed and repeat this
at weekly intervals for *three weeks*. Your pony should then be
clear of worms and all the food you give it will do it good.

After wintering out, when the coat is changing, some ponies
tend to become infested with lice; these must be killed with
Derris powder or one of the proprietary remedies recommended.
Occasionally it is necessary to scrub with a warm solution and
repeat every few days. In this case, the pony must be rugged
up and kept warm, use an old rug and put straw under it until
the pony is dry.

Learn to watch your pony and notice if it looks off colour.
Look out for such things as a filled leg, a loose shoe, a sore back,

28

a girth gall! You will hardly believe it, but many people may have mucked out and groomed the pony, and still not have realised it when something is wrong.

For the filled leg there are two treatments—hot or cold— applied to the leg.

If the filled leg is caused by a thorn, or by any poison which causes inflammation, put on hot Kaolin; you must be able to bear your hand on it, or it will burn. Cover this with cotton wool, mackintosh or brown paper, and then bandage.

If the filled leg is caused by a blow, put on a cold compress with a gamgee tissue or cotton wool, then a bandage. Renew as often as possible. Keep Vaseline in the heels to prevent the dripping water chapping the heel, and always put a supporting bandage on the good leg if the horse is resting the sore one. If you do not do this, the good leg will have to take all the strain unaided.

A sore back needs a lead lotion and then rest, put a numnah or sheepskin under the saddle before the pony is ridden again.

Usually sore backs are caused by an ill-fitting saddle, or by a bad rider who rolls about in the saddle, especially on an unfit pony.

For a girth gall, tie the girth away from the gall, and after bathing the sore, apply a gall ointment.

One other trouble which you should recognise is "colic" or a tummy ache. This may be caused in many ways, and sometimes you can think of no reason for it. The signs are—a restless pony, stamping, looking round at his belly, and in acute stages, sweating from the pain and trying to lie down and roll.

It is wise to keep a colic drench in your stable, but if your pony is bad, you must send for a vet, as it may become very serious and your pony will be in great pain.

CHAPTER FIVE

His Paces and Your Seat

THE horse moves on the diagonal at all paces. Each pace has a different time, but all paces should have rhythm.

For instance, the walk is a pace of four-time—1–2–3–4 not 1–2–34.

The trot is two-time. The canter three-time. The gallop four-time.

The camel, on the other hand, does not move on the diagonal, but paces, i.e. he moves both legs on the same side.

The dog, when galloping, moves with a rotary movement.

To move evenly with a good rhythm, the pony must be re-laxed and supple. The

same is true of the dancer. Once your pony moves in a free relaxed way, in a good rhythm, he becomes a far more comfortable ride.

After he has acquired a good rhythm and goes forward freely with long even strides, he must be taught balance and collection.

30   *The dog galloping moves with a rotary movement*

The horse must be able to extend or collect as his rider wishes.

Balance is learning to shift his and his rider's weight further back. A pony that carries his weight too far forward is said to be unbalanced or "on his forehand".

Collection can only be obtained from the balanced pony, and a pony is said to be collected when he is on the bit and between the rider's legs and hands. His hocks must be under him, and he should be able.and ready to do any movement when he is given the "aid".

The aids—the legs, hands and voice assisted by the artificial aids—the whip, spur and martingale—are the means by which we convey our wishes to the horse.

There is a correct aid for each different movement. These you should be told when you learn to ride, and you must practise applying them correctly and unobtrusively.

The trot is two-time

31

The collected canter

The extended canter

The legs should drive the pony forward, and as they create all the impulsion they are the most important aid.

The hands distribute that impulsion and regulate it. They should be quiet, light and firm, with supple wrists and fingers.

The rider's seat should be balanced and supple. There should be no stiffness; it is impossible to ride well if you are stiff.

Unfortunately one sees so many children's seats spoilt through over-schooling. Too much "sit up straight, heels down, hands held so!"—all before they have learnt a natural balance.

The result is that they ride "all in one piece" looking stiff and inelegant, and the moment the pony shies or bucks they fall off.

The gipsy boy

Not so the gipsy boy; he rides by balance and usually without a saddle. It is true he lacks polish, but he is far better at staying on and with the pony in all circumstances, as he rides by balance and is one with his horse.

Therefore let children first get their natural balance, correcting them as little as possible; let them ride and enjoy themselves on a pony on which they have every confidence. Once they are at home on their ponies, start to drill them and polish them.

Pat Smythe in her book bears out this firm conviction of mine, when she tells us how she rode everywhere on a sheepskin pad without stirrups, and obviously acquired an excellent balance. She also learnt to sit down *into* her pony, and not sit—as so many do—like a stiff little dummy perched on top.

33

Of course the saddle has a lot to do with helping your seat or otherwise, and there are different types of saddles for different jobs.

For yourself, choose a saddle that sits you well into the centre. Study the shape of the seat of the saddles before you buy one. It is a bad fault in riding to sit on the back of your saddle, so don't get the sort of saddle that almost makes you do it!

Different types of saddles are as follows:

1. The English Hunting saddle, which has been used by our fox-hunting ancestors for years. This saddle is much criticized by our foreign friends and by dressage experts as it tends to sit the rider too far back and does not always encourage him to sit *into* his saddle.

2. The Show saddle, which is cut straight in front to show off the horse's shoulder. On some the stirrup bar is set back, to sit the rider even farther back in the saddle.

3. The Show Jumping saddle has a forward cut flap and knee rolls. The padding underneath fits round the rider's leg and lets him sit as comfortably as possible in the position he assumes for jumping. This helps the rider's balance and seat over the obstacles. These saddles are often used with a sheepskin numnah underneath; this is soft to the horse's back and encourages him to round the back and so jump in good style.

4. The Racing saddle, weighing only a few pounds, is used by our flat racing jockeys.

5. The Steeplechase saddle, used with or without a weight cloth, usually has a surcingle, a girth going over the saddle, to help it to stay in place. A breast girth or a breast plate is also used on some horses.

6. The Dressage saddle. The purpose of these saddles is to sit the rider into the centre of the horse. There are many variations,

according to the designs of the different schools of equitation, i.e. Spanish, French, Italian, German, etc. Most of them have a sprung tree and are very comfortable to ride in; they have knee rolls and padding like the jumping saddles, but the stirrup is longer for dressage than for jumping, and the padding is adjusted so that the rider's leg can get as near to the horse as possible.

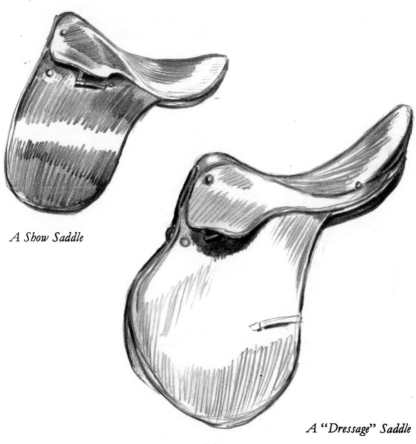

A Show Saddle

A "Dressage" Saddle

Miss D. Mason on Tremella

CHAPTER SIX

Jumping

JUMPING very low obstacles should be part of the early training of both horse and rider.

The rider's body should be supple and with his pony; the hands should be carried low on either side of the pony's neck. Use the legs to get the pony well up to the bit at the trot or canter. As the pony takes off over the fence, allow him to stretch his head and neck by giving your hands, but maintaining contact with the reins; bring your hands back to the normal position as he lands.

You must learn to tell your pony when and where to take off

at each fence. There is a principle of counting three—two, one, OVER—for the three strides when you present your pony at the fence. This you can only learn by constant practice. An extra squeeze is necessary as the take-off signal to your pony. Watch experts jumping and see if you can spot this timing and extra squeeze.

There are numerous ways of schooling jumpers—many excellent and some cruel, but the guiding principle for the ordinary rider is straight forward and clear.

Start with a pole on the ground, lunge your pony over this till he is calm and unfussed, then raise the pole and do the same. Lunge him over all sorts of different-looking obstacles—the more Heath Robinson-looking the better—but always very low. For a young pony, a foot or 18 inches is not too low to start with. Lunge him with the rein fixed to the cavasson ring, or on a

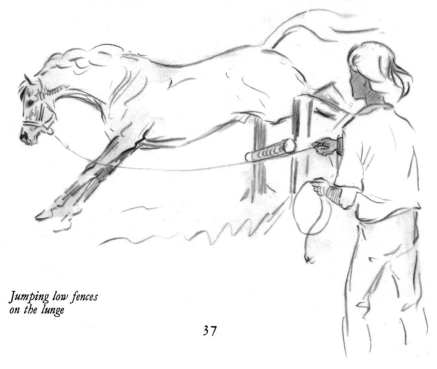

Jumping low fences on the lunge

halter or head collar—never on the bit. Experts can do so if they wish, but this book is not a guide for experts. A jerk in the mouth when jumping will soon put your pony off. Even if it does not stop him jumping, it will make him throw up his head.

Full of confidence

This hollows his back, which lowers his hind quarters, and so spoils the pony's style of jumping, which will make him hit the fence behind.

To jump correctly, the pony must lower his head and neck and get his weight forward. He should look at his take-off—hence the importance of a good ground line, and jump with a rounded back.

He should describe an arc over the obstacle. This is the correct

Major L. Rook on Starlight

style for show jumping and cross country jumping, and you must have this picture in your mind when schooling your pony on the lunge. The jumping in the Grand National is something quite different, magnificent though it is; but you must remember that they can brush through 6 in. to 1 ft. of the National fences, and you have to teach your pony to clear each fence.

When your pony is going well, out hacking, and obeying the aids reasonably well in the school, start riding him over his jumps.

Remember he has got to adjust his balance to carry your weight over the jumps—up to now he has jumped free. Therefore make it easy for him. Start at the beginning over poles on the ground and gradually raise them. Start by riding at all your low jumps out of a trot. Circle round and round, in and out of your jumps—then pop over one, circle again, pop over another two, and so on, always calmly, and reward him when he does well. Let the whole lesson be enjoyable for both of you.

Be sure to have your neck strap in your hand for the first few

Cross Country

lessons. Some youngsters jump very awkwardly, and if you get out of time and left behind over the jump, your hands may fly up, and you risk giving your pony a jab in the mouth.

Wide fences and spreads are better for your pony than lots of upright ones, as they make him extend himself; you can see from the sketches that he will have to jump higher in order to clear the greater widths. This is the best method of schooling your pony to jump heights.

Some wide fences have to be jumped out of a canter. When your pony jumps a varied and low course out of a trot, jump some of the fences out of a canter, then more trotting. He must learn to be completely obedient and jump at whatever pace you wish.

If you start by trotting over low fences, halting and standing still, and then going on over the next fence, you prevent your pony getting hotted up and disobedient. On the other hand, if you start by cantering on at one fence after another before your pony is completely obedient, well-schooled, and handy, he will soon get hotted up and over-keen and start rushing his fences. He is then getting rapidly spoilt.

After you have had a little experience, you will realize that to canter fast round a really twisty course and meet each fence correctly, and to time your jump right, is a very difficult art and wants a high degree of training and practice.

By all means take your pony out hunting—it will be good for both of you. Never school all the time—hack or hunt in between. Galloping on at natural fences will be a good experience for both of you. The good groundwork you have given your pony at home will help him to be clever and handy, and you will both have the greatest fun in the world.

Just one word of warning about jumping while out hunting.

Don't ride a blown pony at fixed timber. Let him get his wind first, otherwise you risk a nasty fall.

Wire is another menace, and you must see that the fence is clear if you get there first, maddening though it may be. Horses can jump wire, and do so; but first they have to be safe clean jumpers, and you must have experience and know what you are doing before you take on wire fences and wire oxers.

When your pony has hunted and has had some experience, take him to shows, hunter trials and rallies. Have as much fun as you like and get all the practice you can, but be careful when jumping not to over face your pony. Ponies can jump incredible heights and enormous fences, but first let them be experienced and full of confidence. This comes in the second year of your training, and you can then launch out and jump in every competition you can get into.

Remember, however good and promising your pony, start the right way and stick to your principles of training. Don't be led astray by people laughing at you, because you will only start him jumping by taking him over small obstacles.

Never be tempted to take on 4 ft. or 5 ft. jumps too soon. Your pony may even jump them once or twice, and then he will begin refusing. Once that happens you have started spoiling him.

Never be tempted to take
on 4 ft. or 5 ft. jumps too soon

CHAPTER SEVEN

The Gymkhana Pony

G YMKHANAS were usually very light-hearted affairs, but nowadays they are often extremely serious.

There is no doubt that these games on horseback can be the greatest fun, but unfortunately they can also become very rough and then they are no fun at all for the ponies.

The original idea of mounted games came from India, and there they were an amusing adjunct to garrison life. However, the soldiers mounts in those days were usually polo ponies, well-balanced and well-schooled and, of course, ideal for bending races and the like.

This should be remembered when you start to train the ideal gymkhana pony.

Looks do not matter, but temperament does. A very "hot" pony, with an excitable temperament, can be difficult, particularly as races tend to excite the pony even more, and it may eventually start fly jumping and becoming almost unmanageable in its excitement—useless when trying to drop a potato into a bucket!

44

A really nervous pony will take a great deal of time and patience, so what is required is a quiet, well-balanced, active animal that will give the rider any amount of fun.

If you are keen and wish to start training your young pony, do not neglect any part of his early training, as to do this will be to spoil the pony and to court disappointment later on.

The pony must learn to carry himself correctly in a snaffle bit and to turn correctly in a balanced manner and until he can do this properly, it is wrong to let him compete in gymkhana events.

If you do this, you will produce the unedifying spectacle of a bewildered, unbalanced pony, being pulled round by the head, and it is this type of rough-riding that often gives gymkhanas a bad name.

When training for all mounted games, start at the walk, and get the pony used to every imaginable object—balloons, umbrellas, washing lines. Be sure to reward him frequently and be quiet and patient until he is not surprised by any type of object.

When you have taken the trouble to school your pony well, and have accustomed him to all the strange sights and sounds, start practising for all the different events, first at the walk, then at the trot, and then at the canter.

The pony must leave the start from a standstill and go straight into a canter, he must change leg like a polo pony, stand like a rock if required, and gallop flat-out for short distances.

All this comes gradually: at your first gymkhana enter only to train the pony and not to win, take the pony quietly and carefully, be sure he understands what you require and do not rush him so that he gets flustered and upset.

Speed and efficiency will come with practice and a great deal is required before you can expect a first-class performance.

Then one word about yourself. A good pony is useless to a child who cannot vault on to a waiting pony and who cannot ride as well without stirrups as with them! Many children these days are no good at riding bare-back or at mounting quickly, this is a great disadvantage and "feeble", so practise until you can do both well!

Learn also the art of throwing straight at an Aunt Sally, and learn the art of bobbing for an apple; it is a knack but you must acquire it before trying to win such a competition.

Be sure your pony looks well and is well turned out and that you are suitably dressed yourself.

The pony should be well trimmed, and great care should be

taken to see that he is well shod. A pony with loose shoes and long toes is more likely to trip and fall than a well-shod animal, and you are asking for trouble if you neglect your pony's feet.

There are also useful rubber bit-guards that can be used on a bit to prevent the pony rubbing the corners of the mouth, often useful when a lot of turning has to be done.

For yourself, always be clean. Gym-shoes are dangerous, as having no heel they can slip through the stirrup-iron, but they are splendid for running if you ride without stirrups, though not of course correct riding-wear! Girls should not wear tight singlets, but wear loose-fitting shirts; these look better on older people, only little children can look attractive in almost anything. Be sure to wear a hard-hat; it is a Pony Club rule and a very wise one too.

Sometimes at shows one sees ponies used as grandstands all day long by their thoughtless owners. Remember the pony needs a rest and a drink and feed in the middle of the day, so see that you bring a halter and either bring or borrow a bucket.

Finally, be a cheerful and sporting competitor and be sure to be a good loser, you will then be a real asset to your team; and good luck to you if you get to the finals at the Horse of the Year Show.

He must also be very well turned out

CHAPTER EIGHT

Showing

IF you intend to go showing, do go about it in the right spirit. It is all a gamble and rather fun, and if you do happen to win, it is better still; but if you don't win, for goodness, sake show a sporting spirit.

The English are famous for their sportsmanship; but to hear some of the spite and jealousy that surrounds the show-ring, one might begin to wonder if it still exists.

Remember always to keep a sense of proportion—a red or blue rosette, and five or ten pounds, or possibly a silver cup are the usual first prizes in pony classes at the larger shows—and to lose this is not a disaster. If you had lost the Derby Stakes, there might be more excuse for your fury!

To win in the show-ring at a good show, a pony must first look well. He must also be very well turned out, and he must be going beautifully. If you are going to show all the summer, and travel about in horse boxes, your pony must be very *fit*, as well as fat and round; so he must have daily exercise—walking exercise to get him fit and turn the fat into muscle. Long days out of the stable are what takes it out of a pony, and travelling miles in a horse box is very tiring; so do try to fit in your feeds early and late to make up the correct amount, and give one feed extra. It may mean getting up at 4 a.m. to feed, if you are leaving at 5 or

5.30. Take haynets for the pony, but do hang them really high up. Rubber buckets are splendid for travelling—try to get one for a present! Don't put heavy rugs on for travelling, or your pony may sweat; but see you have bandages, knee caps, and a tail bandage—a tail guard if possible.

Your turn-out must be excellent; however beautiful your pony, if he is badly turned out, he will not appear at his best.

A nice pony out of condition and shockingly turned out

His mane must be well plaited in very neat plaits, and for this the mane must be pulled short and fairly thin. The ears, heels, and jaw must be well trimmed, and the tail pulled and kept bandaged. The pony's coat must be really well groomed and polished, and a rug will be necessary to keep the coat down and to give the pony that look of finish. A cotton sheet will do in hot weather. Never be tempted to cut at your mane or tail—always pull the hair out, a few hairs at a time. Most ponies do not mind, but for some of them you must have help.

Your saddlery must be smart and it must help your pony's appearance—as your clothes are supposed to help yours. Narrow

Running in hand

leather looks nicer than wide clumsy leather—polish it for showing, if you like. Burnish your bits and stirrup irons, and you can polish your saddle occasionally to make the leather look better; but soap it well before you ride on it, or you will find it rather

Practise your show at home

difficult to sit on. Whiten white socks with chalk and oil the hoofs before you go into the ring.

See that your pony is shod with light shoes—aluminium plates in front are best for showing. No pony can move well if badly shod and wearing heavy clumsy shoes.

School your pony well at home so that he goes at a walk, trot, and canter freely and easily; and pulls up well after his gallop.

Practise his "show" at home—do not try to be too clever—a simple "show" done well is much better than trying something ambitious and making a mess of it. Walk away, trot down, turn and canter back, halt, rein back, and stand still, are quite enough.

Do not try flying changes of leg—it is frowned upon at the big shows—and a simple change, i.e. dropping to a trot in between the change of leg at the canter, is what is required.

See your pony is standing well; this is where your early training is such a help. See that he runs out well in hand. All these things you should practise at home—don't wait for the embarrassing moment to arrive in the ring when you find your pony won't run out in hand, and the ring steward has to shoo him on for you.

To show well, your pony must go like a dancer, balanced and with grace, moving off his hocks and not flopping round the ring on his forehand with his nose stuck out.

Do not go to sleep in the collecting ring or, alternatively, ride

See your pony is standing well

53

the pony about for hours before the class until he is half dead. The pony should have a little exercise before going into the ring, and ponies vary in the amount they need. Be ready to go into the ring well placed. But if someone else is very anxious to go in first, let them do so—there is no point in being unpleasant, and a young pony is better going in behind an old pony, which will give it confidence. Leave several lengths between you and the leader and warn the rider behind you that your pony will kick if she comes too close—so it may, you never know! It is an old dealer's trick to ride too close and so upset your pony and make it go badly, so be warned. If you cannot go in the ring early, go in last, and wherever you are, do not go in in a bunch, and don't get into a bunch once you are in the ring. Do use your wits—don't let anyone cover you up as you go past the judge, and don't do the same mean trick to other people. If you are getting too close to the person in front of you, ride a wider corner than they do. You will then gain several lengths distance, and can go down the straight past the grandstand really well.

If you want to overtake, do so, but on the outside—and don't pass near the other pony, he may kick out. An extended trot is *not* the old butcher boy trot—flat out. If you do this, your pony may put his toe out in front but he also leaves his hocks out behind him. Fatal if he is a bit long in the back! A good ordinary trot is required. Of course, if you have schooled your pony to do a *correct* extended trot, by all means do this when passing the judge. Canter slowly—if you are supposed to gallop, try to see when it is time to gallop and endeavour to be in front—it then *looks* as if your pony is the fastest in the ring, even if it is only an illusion Always ease up round the corners and don't ride someone off into the wing of a jump, even if they are trying to overtake you on the inside.

When in line, don't go to sleep and don't try to be clever and come in out of turn. Remember, ponies are apt to rest a leg when you least want them to. So do be on the alert. By all means talk pleasantly to the competitors on either side of you, but in a very low voice, and not when the judges are coming round.

Wipe your pony down when the saddle is taken off, and see that he stands well on his legs for the judge to look at him. Walk down in a straight line and jog back straight.

When your pony has been looked over, put your saddle on very quickly and get up at once. Be sure to be ready for the next walk round and do it well—it is your *last* chance, so don't miss a moment of it.

A beautiful head is a great help

CHAPTER NINE

Some Ponies of the British Isles

D *ARTMOOR*—One of the smaller native breeds of the British Isles. Stand up to 12.2 h.h. It is a beautiful quality riding pony and is of a sound constitution. They are very hardy, and many herds still run on the moors.

Welsh Mountain—Standing up to 12 h.h. One of the most beautiful of the British native ponies. This hardy little animal is of great antiquity, and although crossed with Arab and Barb horses, it has retained its hardiness and is able to live on the mountains all the year round.

New Forest—not exceeding 14.2 h.h. This pony is a descendant of the ancient pony extant in the British Isles since Palaeolithic times. It has been much "improved" by T.B. and Arab blood and is now a definite type of good riding pony with quality and excellent manners.

Exmoor—This pony is said to be the oldest of the native breeds in Britain and shows definite characteristics of the small horse of the Palaeolithic age. It stands 12.2 h.h. and is a very strong riding pony that is very hardy and possesses tremendous stamina.

Shetland—The smallest of the breeds of the British Isles, standing 10.2 h.h. and under. This tiny pony is tremendously hardy and has survived in the hard conditions of the Shetland Isles for hundreds of years. Formerly used for carrying peat and for all transport by the Islanders, it is now extensively used as a child's riding pony.

Fell—standing 13 h.h. to 14 h.h. Formerly used in the north-west of England to carry lead and coal to the coast, this pony is now an excellent riding pony being hardy and having a good coat. It has a good temperament and a kind disposition.

Dales—A weight-carrying pony, once identical with the Fell pony until Clydesdale blood was crossed into the breed. These ponies lived on the east of the Pennine range in England and were used as pack animals. They stand 14 h.h. and are excellent, hardy riding ponies in the hilly country.

Highland—A beautiful type of weight-carrying pony standing 14.2 h.h. It is used for carrying the deer down from the moors and to carry men in the rough Highland country. It is very sure-footed and is a pleasant balanced ride at slow paces. It is a very strong pony, often carrying stags weighing as much as 20 stone.

Connemara—a native Irish breed of pony standing up to 14.2 h.h. Its origin is pre-history, but it has received many crosses from time to time, among these Barb horses which swam ashore from the wrecked Armada in 1588. The stud-book is now closed to outside blood. A good sound riding pony, hardy and with a good temperament.

Welsh Pony—not exceeding 13.2 h.h. This pony is a quality type of riding pony that has been graded up from the mountain pony.

I have illustrated all these breeds in the following pages.

Dartmoor Ponies.

Welsh Mountain Ponies

New Forest Ponies

Exmoor Ponies

Shetland Ponies

Fell Ponies

Dales Ponies

Highland Ponies

Connemara Ponies

Welsh Ponies .

CHAPTER TEN

In Conclusion

W E have gone quickly through some of the enjoyable things you can do with your pony.

There are many detailed books on every aspect of horsemanship and horsemastership. Read all you can—you will learn something every day, and the more you know, the more interesting life becomes. Never let greed or ambition make you forget to be kind to your animals. If they are hurt, look after them intelligently and devotedly, and remember when they are old, that they have served you well and don't sell them to an unknown end for the few pounds they may fetch. If you cannot afford to pension them off and care for them, and you know of no family who will enjoy having them and will be good to them, then have them destroyed. Always have them put down in the horse-box *before* they leave your yard, it is quick and they can never suffer any more. The Hunt Kennels or the nearest Knacker will do this with a humane killer. Someone you can trust will see to the arrangements for you, but when you have to make the decision, have the courage to do the right thing. If you have ever read *Black Beauty*, the chapter about Poor Ginger will show you what happens when animals go downhill; that, and the pathetic stories of old ponies sold for meat, will make you understand why you have a duty to humanity when you own a dumb creature.

When they have served you well and are old